THE ATHOLE COLLECTION

OF THE DANCE MUSIC OF SCOTLAND

JAMES STEWART ROBERTSON'S
1884 COLLECTION
reprinted with notes on the sources of the tunes

PUBLISHED IN 2008 BY

**HIGHLAND
MUSIC
TRUST**

Arras, Drumossie, Inverness IV2 5BB, Scotland
Tel : 01463 717811   Email : hmt@heallan.com   www.heallan.com

ISBN 978-0-9559306-1-4

Music and text set by Helen Allan   Project managed by Eric Allan
Advisers: Charles Gore, Jim Leslie

Printed in Scotland by Dingwall Printers Ltd

All rights reserved. No part of this publication may be reproduced, stored in a retrieval system or transmitted in any form or by any means without the prior written consent of the publishers.

CONTENTS

Publishers' Note, Preface, Introduction

Original Sources of the Music

	PAGE
Tunes in A major and F♯ minor	1
Tunes in C major and A minor	27
Tunes in D major and B minor	52
Tunes in G major and E minor	84
Tunes in B♭ major and G minor	114
Tunes in F major and D minor	135
Tunes in E♭ major and C minor	161
Tunes in E major	167
Hornpipes	169
Jigs	172
Country Dances	176
Index	183
Gaelic Titles and Translations	189

PUBLISHERS' NOTE

In reproducing this important collection, we pay tribute to Balnain House, Inverness, which until its unfortunate closure did so much for Scottish music, including the reprint of the Athole Collection in 1996.

We have preserved the principle of grouping of tunes in the same key, extending it to combine major and relative minor keys and incorporating into that system the tunes in the Addenda to the 1884 edition. We have moved a few tunes to more appropriate key sections, and have applied a light editorial hand to the notes only where necessary. The alphabetical indices and notes of Gaelic names from the original two-volume publication have been combined and the bass lines of the tunes have been omitted. We acknowledge the work of the late Fred Macaulay in revising the Gaelic titles. We are grateful to the family of the late Duke of Atholl and to Alasdair Fraser for permission to reproduce the preface and introduction to the Balnain House edition.

Such was the outpouring of published music both in the "Golden Age" and also more-or-less contemporaneously with the 1884 collection that almost all of the tunes also appeared elsewhere. The exceptions are: those marked JSR (composed by James Stewart Robertson) and a few by his contemporaries; tunes not identified elsewhere that he may have collected from contemporary sources; and others marked simply *Reel* or *Strathspey* which appear elsewhere in other versions not instantly comparable. In order to give some perspective to the tunes, we have for the first time included notes on the sources of the tunes, for which we are most indebted to Charles Gore, compiler of the monumental *Scottish Fiddle Music Index*. As he has pointed out, this task can never be complete, and is complicated by apparent similarities in some of the tunes, but by opening the doors to the great library of Scottish music, we hope that readers will venture in.

Thanks are due to Charles Gore, Jim Leslie and Duncan Dyker for their continuing support.

HIGHLAND MUSIC TRUST is a Scottish Charity, No. SC028065, established for the advancement of education in and knowledge of Scottish national and traditional music. The proceeds of this book will be used to continue the work of the Trust in making music available to all. Information on the Trust's publications may be had from the address on the previous page or the Trust's website www.heallan.com.

PREFACE TO THE 1996 EDITION
by His Grace the Duke of Atholl DL

I am pleased to welcome the republication of this major collection of the dance music of Scotland. It is a work which has long been known to and respected by scholars, but has not been readily available to musicians and the general public. In the current climate of healthy interest in traditional arts, I am sure that this publication will be greeted with enthusiasm and will prove to be a valuable source of information, and inspiration, to all those interested in our musical heritage. I commend the initiative of Balnain House Trust in its contribution to the living tradition of Scottish music.

INTRODUCTION TO THE 1996 EDITION
by Alasdair Fraser

I have great pleasure in being asked to write an introduction for this timely reprint of the Athole Collection (1884) by James Stewart Robertson. Described by Francis Collinson in his foreword to the 1961 edition as an "Encyclopaedia of Scottish Dance Music", this collection of tunes has been a great source of inspiration and joy to me as a working musician and teacher in the Scottish dance music and performance field.

The "revival of interest" in Scottish Dance music observed by Collinson in 1960 has continued unabated. Many young Scots find this music to be a very satisfactory means of expression in the changing world of the last days of the twentieth century. Outwith Scotland, performances and recordings of Scottish traditional music continue to increase in popularity.

James Stewart Robertson of Edradynate, Perthshire, was a founding member of Edinburgh Highland Reel and Strathspey Society and became President of that organisation in 1881. At that time interest in Scottish fiddle music seemed to be in decline and Robertson is quoted in the society's minutes as saying that it was "very desirable that this class of music should not be allowed to fall back as undoubtedly it was doing for the past few years" [*Mary Ann Alburger: Scottish Fiddlers and their Music*]. The Athole Collection was published three years later in 1884. It contains 870 strathspeys, reels, jigs, hornpipes and country dances and creates an extremely high quality cross section of the Scottish fiddle repertoire up until that time. As Collinson points out, the author was able to cull from the many previously published collections of the eighteenth and nineteenth centuries such as those of Niel and Nathaniel Gow, William Marshall and Captain Simon Fraser.

A unique aspect of Robertson's approach, however, is that he has included many ornamentation and phrasing ideas which are of great value to the player who is less familiar with the Scottish musical idiom. The original edition included a rudimentary accompaniment for the piano left hand or bass, as was the fashion in some of the older collections. In view of the evolving and dynamic nature of accompaniment in traditional music, a decision has been made by the editors of this current edition to allow these tunes to continue their journey into the twenty first century in their earlier "untethered" state.

Alasdair Fraser, California, June 1996.

ORIGINAL SOURCES OF THE MUSIC IN THE ATHOLE COLLECTION

AIRD, James (Glasgow)	"A Selection ..." 1782; vols 2-6 1780s-c1801
ANDERSON, John (Edinburgh)	From 1790, but there may more than one of the name
BAYNE, Charles (Dundee)	Sets of dances 1802-1819
BOWIE, John (Perth)	Collection 1789
BOWIE, Peter (Perth)	Collection 1806
BREMNER, Robert (Edinburgh/London)	14 "instalments" from 1761; other (later) collections
CAMERON, George (Glasgow)	Selection of Violin Music 1854
CAMPBELL, Joshua (Glasgow)	Four Collections from c1786
* CHRISTIE, William (Cuminestown)	1778-1849; Collection 1820
CLARKSON, John, Jnr. (Edinburgh)	Collection 1803
CLARKSON, John, Snr. (London)	2 Collections from c1796
* COOPER, Isaac (Banff)	2 collections c1783 and c1806
* CUMMING, Angus (Grantown-on-Spey)	Collection 1780; helped promote the "strathspey reel"
DOW, Daniel (Perthshire)	1732-83; 4 collections from c1773
DUFF, Archibald (Montrose)	2 collections, 1794 and 1811/12
EGLINTON, 12 Earl of (Ayrshire)	1739-1819; Collection 1796 (Nath. Gow)
*** FRASER, Capt. Simon ("of Knockie")	"New & Old Tunes" 1795; Major work 1816 & 1874
FRENCH, John (Ayr)	Collection (posthumous) Edinburgh 1801
GALE'S Pocket Companion	Glasgow, in two parts (from 1800) Many song airs
GOW & Sons	Gow Bks 5-6; Complete Repository, vols 1-4 1799 -
GOW & Sons	Beauties of Gow vols 1-3 1819
GOW, John & Andrew	Sons of Niel Gow; Collection from c 1793
GOW, Nathaniel (Edinburgh)	Publisher of his own and other composers' collections
GOW, Niel, at Dunkeld	GOW Bks 1-4 First Editions 1784-1800
* GRANT, Charles (Aberlour)	1810-92 Coll. (posthumous & privately printed)
* GRANT, Donald (Elgin)	1760-1839; Collection 1780
HALL, John (Ayr)	1788-1862; Collection 1818
JOHNSON, Abraham (Edinburgh)	Collection c1795
LADIES/LADY (various)	3 collections, two pub. by Nath.Gow 1796 & c1798
MAC(K)INTOSH, Abraham	Son of Red Rob; 3 colls.(one pub: Newcastle, c1805)
** MACDONALD, Malcolm (Dunkeld)	4 collections 1788-1797; "Played bass to Niel Gow"
MacGLASHAN, Alexander	Edinburgh 1740-97; 3 collections 1778, 1781, 1788
MACKAY, Alexander (Islay)	Collection c1805
* MACKINTOSH, Robert ("Red Rob")	c.1745-1807; 4 important collections from 1783
* MARSHALL, William (Fochabers)	2 major and 2-3 minor collections from 1781
McFADYEN, Joseph (Glasgow)	2 Collections c1800 and c1802; publisher
McGIBBON William (Edinburgh)	2 Collections 1755 in 3 books; 1768 in 4 books
McINTYRE, Duncan (London)	c.1765-1807 Col; 1795 plus attributions elswhere
McKERCHER, Duncan (Dunkeld)	2 full collections c1830; Lived a while in Inver
McLAREN, Daniel (? Born Taymouth)	Collection 1794 Edinburgh
MENZIES, Capt Daniel (Perth)	May have composed much of McKercher's music
MIDDLETON Charles (Keith)	1837-1899; Several collections; see MILNE, Peter
MILNE, Peter (Tarland)	Edited Middleton's collection containing his work
MORISON, Jane Fraser (Kintail)	2 vols "Highland Airs ..." 1882
MORISON, John (Peterhead)	Collections c1797 and c1815
* MORRISON, William (Inverness)	Collection 1812; much of his own work
NAPIER, William	1740-1812; 2 Collections 1790-94 and 1798
OSWALD, James (Fife/London)	Prolific publisher of songs airs etc. from 1735
PETRIE, Robert (Perthshire)	4 collections partly his own 1790-1805 Kirkmichael
PRINGLE, John (Edinburgh)	2 Collections 1801 Published together (?)

REINAGLE, Alexander (Edinburgh)	Collection 1782
RIDDELL (Riddle), John (Ayr)	Collection c.1766, re-published ("improved") 1782
RIDDELL, Capt. Robert (of Glenriddell)	2 Collections 1787 & 1794; Friend of Robt. Burns
SHEPHERD, William (Edinburgh)	2 Collections 1793 & c1800; worked with Nath. Gow
SKILLERN, Thomas (London)	Dance Manual 1780, a very rare book
SKINNER, James Scott	Banchory, 1848-1927; Many well-known publications
STEWART, Charles (Edinburgh)	c.1770-1818; 2 collections 1799/20 and 1805
STEWART, Neil (Edinburgh)	1730-c1815; Prolific publisher from 1761
STIRLING, Miss Magdalina	Ardoch, Perthshire. "12 Tunes ..." (her own, c 1800)
* WALKER, James (Dysart)	2 Collections 1797 & 1800

LATER SOURCES

* GLEN, John (Edinburgh)	2 volumes of dance music 1891 & 1895
KERR, James S. (Glasgow)	4 volumes "Merrie Melodies for the Violin" 1870
LOWE, Joseph (Edinburgh)	Books 1-6 and Royal Collection (2 vols) from 1844
*** MacDONALD Dr Keith Norman (Skye)	"The Skye Collection" 1887

Compiled by Charles Gore
Doune, Perthshire April 2008

* Republished by Highland Music Trust
** Republished by Taigh na Teud
*** Republished by P S Cranford

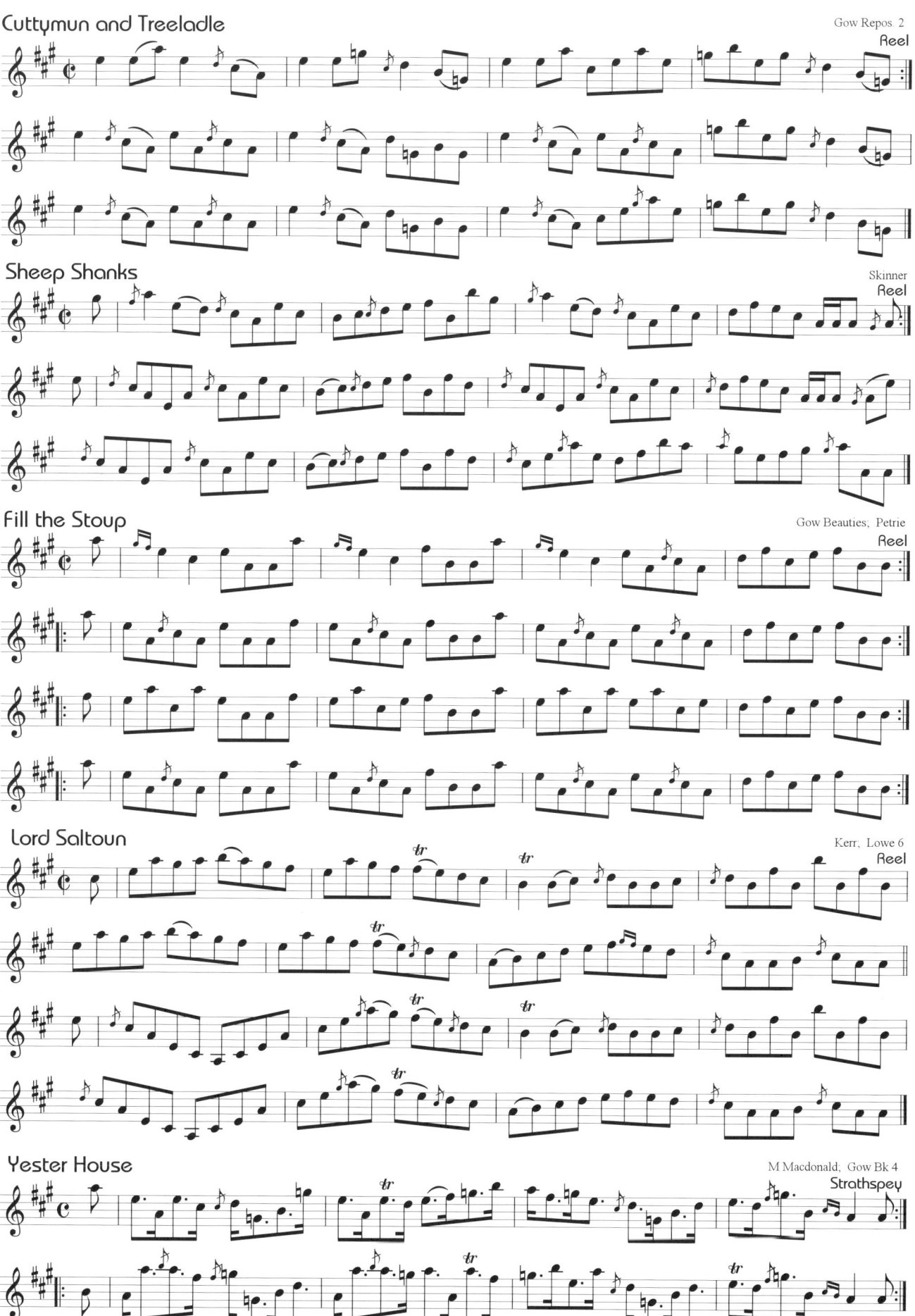

Tunes in C Major and A Minor

* cf. Highland Watch - Gow Repos. 2

Deil Tak the Breeks *

Reel

cf. O Grain air na Briogaisean - S Fraser

Miss Mary Stewart of Derculich

R Petrie
Reel

The Auld Stewart's Back Again

Lowe
Reel

Cheap Meal
R Mackintosh 3; Lowe; Kerr 1
Reel

Carrick's Rant *
Bremner
Strathspey

* cf. The Smith's a Gallant Fireman

Lady Mary Stopford *
Gow Bk 4; Lowe; Kerr 3; Skye
Reel

* Lady Mary Montague (Glen)

Lads of Tain
Lowe; Skye; Kerr 2
Strathspey

This Is No' My Ain House
Gow Bk 1; Kerr 1; Skye
Reel

Alexander Brodie *

*Mrs Alexander Brodie's Reel (D Grant)

Lord John Campbell

Miss Johnston *

*Miss Johnson of Byker's Reel (R Mackintosh)

The Uist Lasses' Darling *

*Mac a' Bhaillidh á Uist (S Fraser)

The Moray Club

Tunes in G Major and E Minor

*cf. Will you go to Sheriff Muir (Bremner)

* cf. Mrs McDonnell of Lochgarry's Reel (McKercher)

* Cropie's Strathspey (Middleton/Milne)

* Miss Pensy Macdonald's Reel (Gow Bk 2) [see page 102]

* Lady Belhaven's Reel (Gow Bk 2) [see page 96]

* cf. Drummore's Rant - Bremner

The Glenburney Rant *
Reel

* *The Glenburnie Rant (Gow Bk 5); Small (Sma') Coals for Nailers (Kerr 4; Middleton)*

Delvine Side
MacGlashan, Skinner
Strathspey

Tarbolton Lodge *
Kerr 1
Reel

* *Hatton Burn (Skye)*

Colonel Baird
Anderson
Strathspey

*Mrs Fleming of Moness (Gow Bk 1; Glen; Skye)

Miss Hog, Newliston — R Mackintosh 3 — Reel

Miss Mary Macdonald * — Reel

* cf. Mrs Fraser of Culduthel's Strathspey (S Fraser vol. 1)

The Braes of Tullymet — Gow Repos. 1, Skye — Strathspey

The Hon. George Carnegie — D McLaren — Strathspey

Miss Austin * — Strathspey

* Miss Oustein's Strathspey (M McDonald 3)

The Duchess of Gordon
Gow Repos. 3 — Strathspey

Miss Ann Stewart, East Craigs *
Reel

* cf. Strathspey Gow Bk 2; Skye

The Weaver's Daughter
Kerr 3 — Strathspey

Tunes in F Major and D Minor

The Cameronian Rant
Bremner, Lowe, Skye 1 — Reel

135

*Lord Glenorcha's Strathspey

Duchess of Bedford *
Reel

* cf. Lady Georgina Gordon's Strathspey (Marshall)

Miss Welsh
Gow Bk 5
Reel

'Stoigh leam féin an Siosalach - The Chisholm
S Fraser
Strathspey

Miss Macpherson Grant of Ballindalloch *
Strathspey

* Miss Isabella McPherson Grant's Strathspey - of Ballindalloch (Marshall)

Lord Hum's Reel (Anderson)

Caileagan a' Bhaille Mhòr (S Fraser)

Mrs Gordon of Belsies *

Slow Strathspey

*Mrs Gordon of Bellie's Strathspey (Marshall; Gow Repos. 3)

Lady Georgina Gordon

R Mackintosh 3
Reel

Mr Bernard

Gow Bk 5; Lowe
Reel

148

*Mrs J W Bourke's Reel (Gow Bk 4)

* *The Forest of Garth*

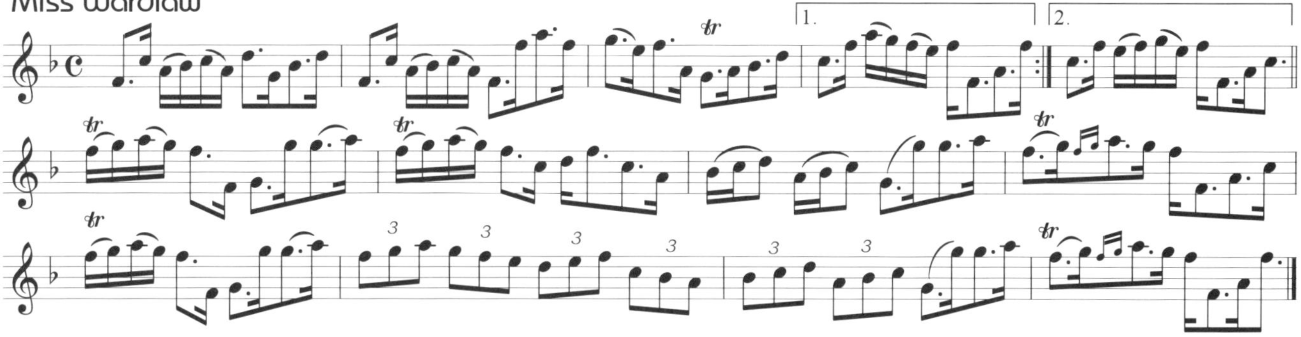

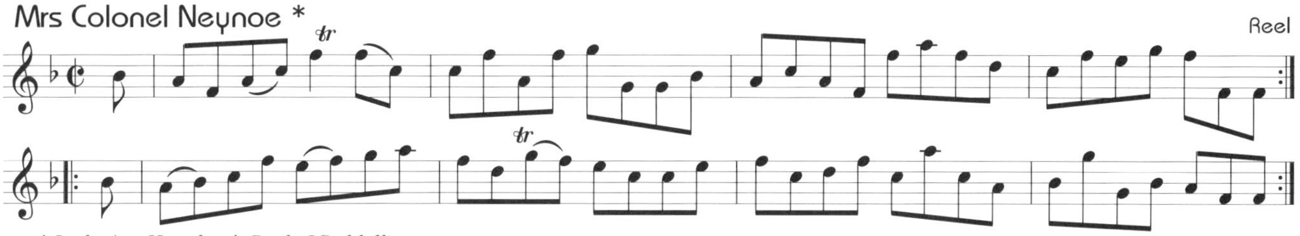

Tunes in E Major

Mr Dundas Macqueen
Gow Bk 2 — Reel

Duchess of Gordon *
Skye — Strathspey

* cf. The Dutchess of Gordon's Strathspey (Dow)

The Belted Plaid and Health to Wear it *
Reel

* Am breacan ùr gum meal thu e (S Fraser)

John Angus *
Reel

*Mr John Angus's Reel - of Calcutta; [cf. Johnston's Reel, A Strathspey] (Marshall)

Gorthleck's Highland Plaid *

Strathspey

* *Breacan ùr Fhir Ghortuileic (S Fraser)*

Miss Muir Mackenzie

Gow Bk 5
Strathspey

Eclipse

Kerr 2

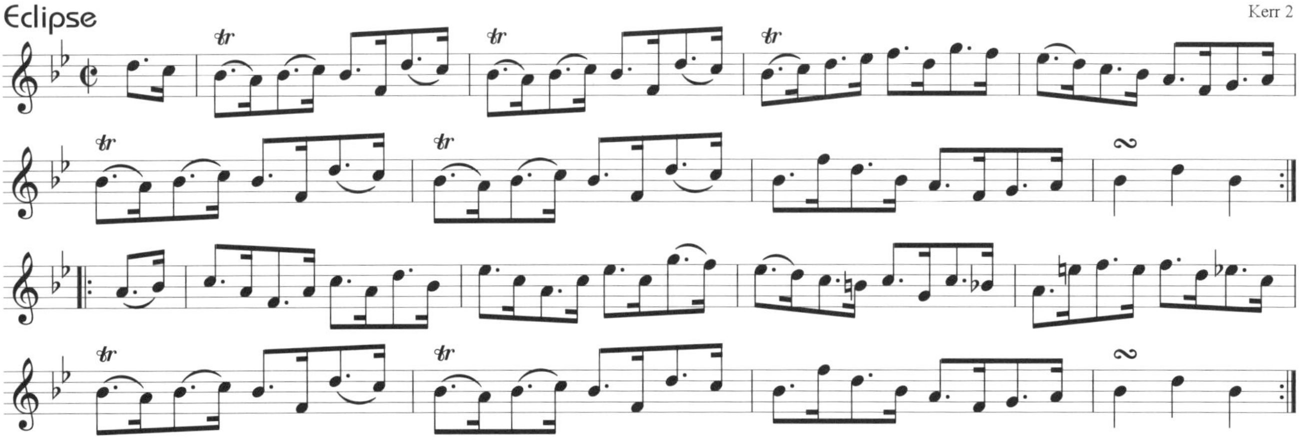

Morpeth Rant

Koehler

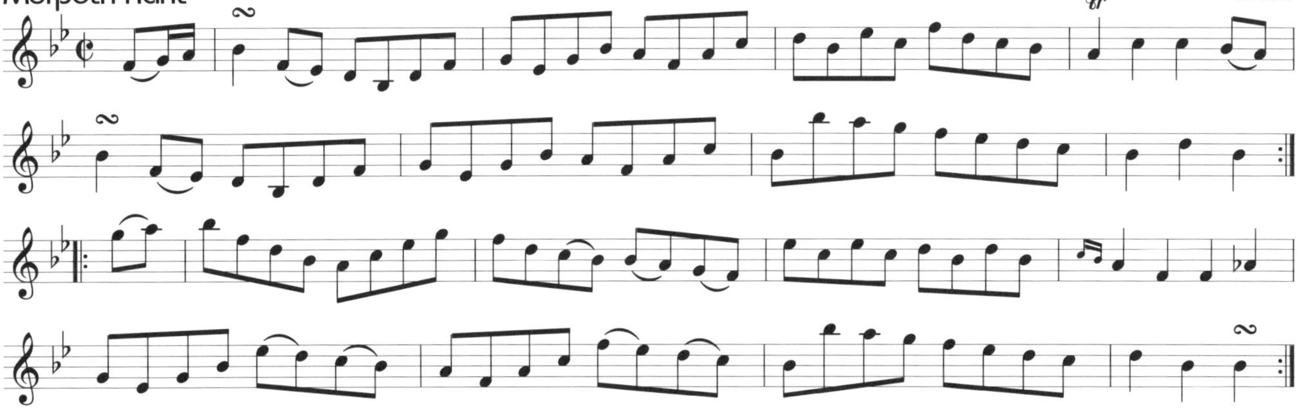

Jigs

Teviot Bridge

Gow Repos 4; Kerr 1; Skye

The Stool of Repentance

Gow Bk 5; Lowe; Kerr 3

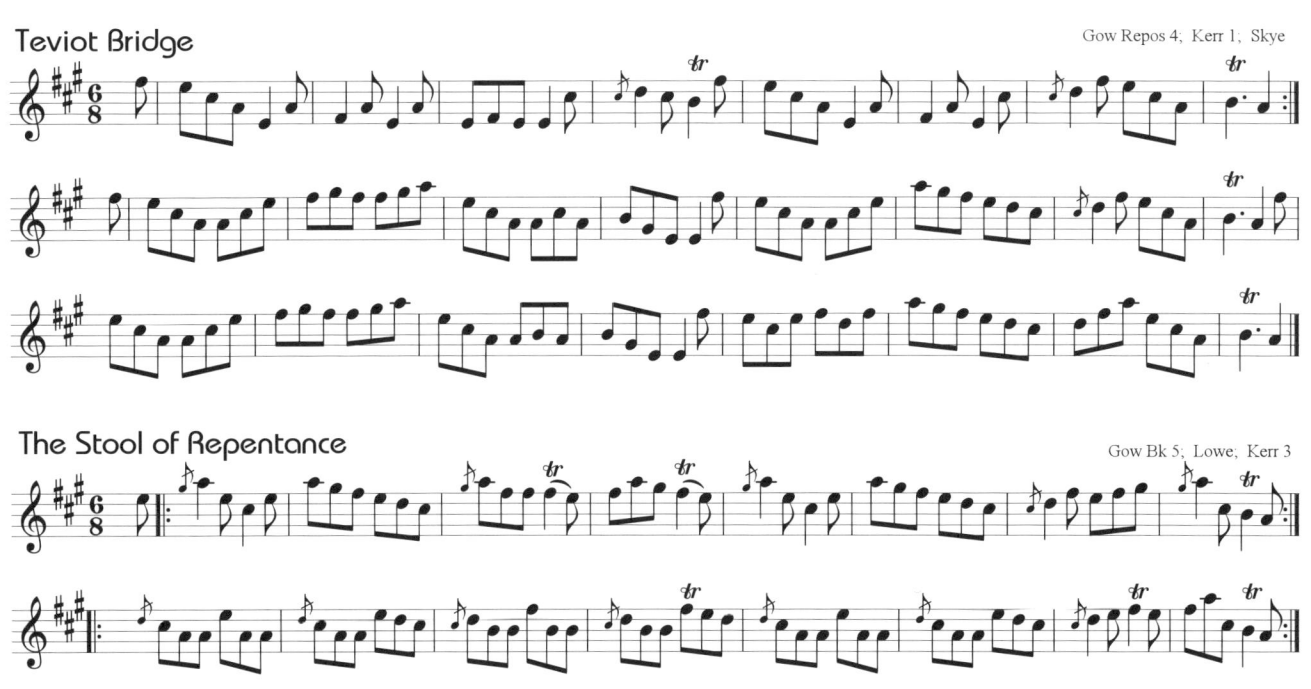

Lads of Dunse

My Wife's A Wanton Wee Thing

The General Gathering 1745 *

An Cruinneachadh iomlan luthmhor (S Fraser)

Lady Nelly Wemyss

Prince Charlie's Medley *

Danced at Holyrood, 1745

Country Dances

Johnny Macgill
J Campbell; Skye

The Breeks Are Loose and the Button's Awa' *

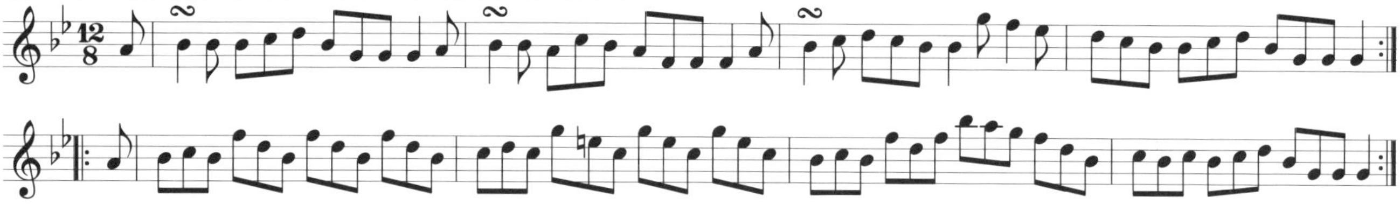

* The Breeches Maker (Gow Bk 4)

The Triumph
G Cameron; Skye, Kerr 1

Meg Merrilees
G Cameron, Lowe; Kerr 1

Willie Davie
Lowe, Kerr 1

INDEX

A' Chridhealachd – or The Merry Making	136
A' Chuachag	67
A Dhomhnuill, A Dhomhnuill	87
Abercairny House	166
Aberdeen Hunt	132
Aberlour's Squeeze	27
Alasdair MacAlasdair	43
Alexander Brodie	73
Allt A' Ghobhainn – or The Smith's Burn	3
Am Bodach Luideach Odhar	63
Ambulree	96
America – or Null Thar Nan Eileanan	6
An Gabh Thu Bean, A Dhò'ill Bhig! – or Little Donald's Wife	42
An Gearran	53
An Gille Dubh, Mo Laochan	53
An Oidhche a Bha Bhanais Ann - or The Lea Rig	5
An Oidhche Bha Na Gabhair Againn – or The Night We Had The Goats	92
Andrew Carr	174
Anna Is My Darling	11
Appin House	1
Archduke John of Austria	141
Argyle Bowling Green	31
Arthur's Seat	81
As A Thòiseach	106
Athole Brose	75
Athole Cummers	107
Athole House	140
Athole Lads	7
Athole's Bonnie Lasses	98
Athole's Honest Man	98
Auchtertyre House	78
Auld Lang Syne	1
Auld Stewart's Back Again, The	64
Auld Stewarts of Forthergill	29
Auld Toun o' Ayr, The	70
Ayrshire Lasses	30
Back of the Change House, The	63
Baile Nan Granndach	75
Ballechin Rant	59
Ballindalloch's Dream	46
Balmoral Castle	91
Banks of Garry, The	72
Banks of Loch Ness, The	128
Beauty of the North, The	163
Because He Was A Bonny Lad	7
Bedding of the Bride, The	75
Belfast Almanac, The	175
Belladrum House	65
Belted Plaid and Health to Wear It, The	167
Ben Lomond	57
Ben Nevis	63
Biodag Air Mac Alasdair	19
Biodag Air MacThòmais	2
Biodag Dhò'ill-Ic Alasdair - or Glengarry's Dirk	14
Birks of Aberfeldy	139
Black But Comely	61
Blair Drummond	101
Blue Bonnets Over the Border	15
Blue Bonnets Ow'r the Border	178
Bob O' Dooly, The – or Port Nan Con	8
Bob of Fettercairn, The	89
Bobers of Brechin, The – or The Strathbogie Toast	127
Bog o' Gight, The	9
Bonfire, The	129
Bonnie Annie	42
Bonny Lass of Ballantrae	137
Bonny Lass of Fisherrow	33
Bonny Lassie O'	162
Bonny Toun 'o Kenmore, The	88
Bottom of the Punch Bowl, The	180
Braes of Athole, The	100
Braes of Auchtertyre	28
Braes of Balquhidder	141
Braes of Mar (Old Set), The	55
Braes of Mar (Reel)	53
Braes of Mar (Strathspey)	53
Braes of Tullymet, The	125
Brandlings	19
Brechin Castle	114
Breeks Are Loose and the Button's Awa', The	176
Bridge of Bamore	2
Bridge of Garry, The	13
Bridge of Inver, The	118
Bridge of Perth	14
Brig o' Balater, The	32
Brig o' Dee, The	58
Brig o' Tilt, The	65
Briogan Seambo	85
Brisk Bob	82
Brodie of Brodie	72
Broun's Reel	30
Buck of the Cabrach, The	80
Ca' the Stirks	50
Ca' Hawkie Through the Water – or Lord Elphinston	49
Cabar-Féidh	27
Caisteal Chuimri	90
Caithness Rant, The	165
Calabria	149
Calum Breugach	48
Calum Figheadair	151
Cameronian Rant, The	135
Cameron's Got His Wife Again	52
Captain Byng	90
Captain Campbell	46
Captain David Stewart 42nd Royal Highlanders	71
Captain Elphinston	124
Captain Fife	155
Captain George Hunter	81
Captain H. Munro	134
Captain Keeler	134
Captain Macduff's Farewell	112
Captain McDuff	14
Captain Ross	14
Carle Cam' O'er The Craft, The	12
Carlisle Lasses	155
Carn Dubh	8
Carrick's Rant	66
Catch and Kiss the Romp	40
Cawdor Fair	42
'Chailleach Mhùsgach – or The Drunken Wife	19
'Chailleach Odhar – or The Dunn Carline	54
'Chailleach Oidhche	22
Charles Leslie	71
Charlie Stewart	57
Cheap Meal	66
Cheap Mutton – or Coille An Togail	127
Chisholm, The – or 'Stoigh leam féin an Siosalach	142
Chuir I Glùn Air A' Bhodach	46
Ciorsdan Mhór (Reel) – or Miss Stewart, Bunrannoch	113
Ciorsdan Mhór (Strathspey)	112
Clach Na Cùdain	60
Clanranald	112
Cluny Rock	21
Clydesdale Lasses	152
Cock of the North, The	116
Coille An Togail - or Cheap Mutton	127
Coirechoille	82
Colbeck House	32
Collar Green	102
College Hornpipe	171
Colonel Baird	103
Colonel Fraser of Knocky	93
Colonel Macbean	126
Colonel Montgomery	57
Colonel Robertson	113
Colonel Thornton	41
Colonel Wemyss	153
Colquhalzie Fir Trees	99
Come Along and Keep Your Promise	162
Comely Garden	7
Coopers Hornpipe	169
Corimonie's Rant	56
Corn Rigs	179
Cottar's Wife, The	26

Count D'Artois	38
Countess of Breadalbane	123
Countess of Cassillis	18
Countess of Dalhousie	149
Countess of Rothes, The	151
Countess of Sutherland	120
County Hall	90
Craig O' Barns	130
Craigellachie Bridge	62
Craigie Hall	70
Creag Na Pollaich	31
Crieff Fair	158
Crònan Na Linne Mhuilich – or Sound of Mull	43
Cross of Inverness, The	98
Croughly	157
Cullen House	72
Culloden House	166
Cumberland, The – or Miss Gibson	114
Cut and Dry	16
Cut Him Down Susie	58
Cuttie's Wedding	50
Cutting Ferns	51
Cuttymun and Treeladle	17
Dainty Davie	139
Dalkeith House	71
Dalry House	67
Darling, The	26
Dashing White Sergeant, The	181
Dawted Mary	83
Deer Forest, The	150
Deil Amang the Tailors, The	6
Deil Tak the Breeks	64
Delvine Side	103
Dervaig Medley, The – or Old Isle of Mull Tune	174
Deuk's Dang O'er My Daddie, The	178
Doctor, The	115
Dogs Bite Chapmen	62
Dòmhnull Cléireach	74
Don Side	91
Donald Dow – or Lady Charlotte Murray	150
Donald MacGugan's Rant	67
Donald Quaich	45
Double Kisses	30
Douglas Hornpipe	171
Dr Gregory Grant	78
Dr Manson of Spynie	158
Druim-Uachdair	86
Drumins	80
Drummer, The	42
Drummond's Rant	102
Drunken wife, The – or 'Chailleach Mhùsgach	19
Drunken Wives of Fochabers, The	134
Dubh Chnocan	61
Duchess of Bedford	142
Duchess of Gordon	167
Duchess of Gordon, The	67
Duchess of Gordon, The	135
Duchess of Hamilton	87
Duchess' Slipper, The	98
Duff of Muirtown	100
Duke of Athole, The	48
Duke of Cumberland	65
Duke of Gordon's Birthday, The	89
Duke of Kent	147
Duke of Perth	93
Dumfries House	175
Duncan Davidson	59
Duncan McQueen	51
Dunfermline Races	11
Dunie Mains	86
Dunkeld Bridge	147
Dunkeld Hermitage	110
Dunn Carline, The – or 'Chailleach Odhar	54
Dunrobin Castle	121
Duns Dings A'	12
Dunt the Grund at Leisure	88
Earl Grey	3
Earl Marischal	146
Earl of Breadalbane	105
Earl of Dalhousie	164
Earl of Dalkeith	152
Earl of Eglinton's Birthday	155
Earl of Home	145
Earl of Hyndford	163
Earl of Lauderdale, The	96
Earl of Loudon	149
Earl of March	141
East Neuk of Fife	179
Easter Elchies	158
Eclipse Hornpipe	172
Edradynate House (Reel)	55
Edradynate House (Strathspey)	54
Edradynate Medley	182
Evans Hornpipe	170
Ewie Wi' the Crooked Horn	11
Ewie Wi' the Crooked Horn	129
Fair Fa' the Minstrel	115
Fairy Dance, The	72
Fang the Fiddlers	47
Feargan	43
Feet Washing, The	162
Ferintosh	65
Fife Hunt	35
Fight About the Fireside	29
Fill the Stoup	17
Fishers Hornpipe	169
Fisher's Rant, The	92
Fisher's Wedding, The	143
Flagon, The	92
Flora Macdonald – or Theàrlaich! Nan Tigeadh Tu!	104
Flowers of Edinburgh	178
Forest of Gaick, The	156
Forfar Hunt	82
Fox Chase	23
Francis Sitwell	117
Fraser Arms, The	121
Fyket, The (Reel)	24
Fyket, The (Strathspey)	24
Gabhaidh Sinn an Rathad Mór – or The Stewart's March	181
Garey Cottage	143
Garthlands	95
General Gathering 1745, The	173
General Macdonald	37
General Macdonald	164
General Wemyss of Wemyss	31
Gille Calum	4
Gin I Had a Bonny Lassie	128
Glasgow Lasses	144
Glen Ogle	60
Glenburney Rant, The	103
Glenelg	62
Glengarry's Dirk - or Biodag Dhò'ill-Ic Alasdair	14
Glenlyon	46
Glenlyon	68
Glenmoriston	97
Glenquey	80
Glentilt	2
Glentromie	39
Golden Locks	82
Gordon Castle	12
Gordons Hae the Girding O't, The	70
Gorthleck's Highland Plaid	168
Grant Lodge	99
Grantully Bridge	124
Green Grow the Rashes O!	85
Greig's Pipes	10
Haggis of Dunbar, The	25
Haggis, The – or Taigeis Agus Dealg Innte	29
Harvest Home (Hornpipe)	170
Harvest Home (Strathspey)	52
Haste to the Wedding	177
Haughs of Cromdale	104
High Road to Fort Augustus	83
High Road to Linton	21

High Up the Glen	131
Highland Dress and Armour	36
Highland Skip, The	143
Highland Whisky	3
Highlander's Farewell to Ireland, The	45
Highlandman Kissed His Mother, The	47
Highlands of Banffshire, The	143
Hilton Lodge	33
Hoch Hey Johnnie Lad	16
Hon. Captain Maitland	93
Hon. George Carnegie, The	125
Hon. John Leslie Melville	157
Hon. Miss Drummond of Perth, The	69
Hon. Mr Ramsay Maule	111
Hon. Mrs Graham of Balgowan, The	69
Hon. Mrs Maule	20
Hon. Mrs Maule of Panmure	153
Honble Miss Drummond of Perth	10
Honest Duncan	120
Honey Moon, The	74
Honourable Peace, An	108
House of Achluncart, The	40
House of Cluny, The	147
House of New, The	40
House of Park, The	156
Hurdle Race, The	21
I Winna Gae to Bed	61
II Ye Had Been Where I Hae Been	72
I'll Gang Nae Mair to Yon Town	136
I'll Hap Ye In My Plaidie	105
I'll Mak' Ye Be Fain to Follow Me	175
Inver Lasses	11
Invercauld	47
Inverness Lasses	145
Irish Washerwoman	174
Irvine Steeple	80
Island of Java	39
Isle of Skye	114
Jack a' Tar Hornpipe	169
James McNicoll	30
Jenkins Hornpipe	171
Jenny Dang the Weaver	53
Jenny Drinks Nae Water	180
Jenny Nettles	177
Jenny Sutton	18
Jenny's Bawbee	56
Jessie Smith	54
Jinglin Johnnie	177
John Angus	167
John Cheap, the Chapman	128
John McAlpin	2
John Roy Stewart	138
Johnnie Lad	104
Johnnie Pringle	86
Johnnie's Made a Waddin' O't	101
Johnny Groat's House – or Tigh Iain Ghròit	36
Johnny Macgill	176
Keel Row	6
Keep the Country Bonny Lassie	15
Kenmore Lads	178
Kids, The	24
Killiechassie	94
Killin	12
Kincaldrum	94
King George IV's Welcome	42
King's, The	42
Kinrara (Reel)	140
Kinrara (Strathspey)	122
Kiss Me Fast	174
Knockando House	80
Ladar Mór A'Ghogain	106
Lads o' Elgin, The	41
Lads of Duns	173
Lads of Foss, The	58
Lads of Tain	66
Lady Amelia Murray	77
Lady Ann Hope	86

Lady Ann Hope	95
Lady Ashburton	164
Lady Baird	4
Lady Belhaven	96
Lady Binning	5
Lady Burnside's Birthday	165
Lady Carmichael	29
Lady Caroline Montague	35
Lady Charlotte Campbell (Reel)	116
Lady Charlotte Campbell (Strathspey)	94
Lady Charlotte Campbell (Strathspey)	116
Lady Charlotte Durham	11
Lady Charlotte Menzies	145
Lady Charlotte Murray	77
Lady Charlotte Murray – or Donald Dow	150
Lady Charlotte Primrose	76
Lady Doune	136
Lady Down	27
Lady Dumfries	145
Lady Elizabeth Campbell	21
Lady Elizabeth Lindsay	117
Lady Georgina Gordon	148
Lady Georgina Russell	122
Lady Glenorchy	20
Lady Grace Douglas	119
Lady Grace Stewart	84
Lady Hamilton Dalrymple	131
Lady Hampden	25
Lady Harriet Hope	143
Lady Helen Wedderburn	78
Lady Jane Montgomery	154
Lady Jane Neville	88
Lady Jane Taylor	34
Lady Jardine	144
Lady Jemima Johnston	37
Lady Loudon	30
Lady Lucinda Ramsay	131
Lady Lucy Leslie Melville	154
Lady Lucy Ramsay	31
Lady Madalina Gordon	157
Lady Madelina Sinclair	6
Lady Madelina Sinclair's Birthday	117
Lady Margaret Stewart	84
Lady Mary Hope Vere	69
Lady Mary Menzies	159
Lady Mary Murray	96
Lady Mary Ramsay	55
Lady Mary Ramsay	164
Lady Mary Stopford	66
Lady Montgomery	114
Lady Nelly Wemyss	173
Lady of the Lake	178
Lady Shaftesbury	165
Lady Spencer Chichester	150
Lady Susan Gordon	123
Laird of Macintosh, The	95
Lamberton Races	152
Largo Law	18
Lasses' Fashion, The	22
Lasses Like Nae Brandy	13
Lasses of Stewarton, The	60
Lassie Look Before Ye	63
Lassie Look Behind Ye	55
Lassie Wi' the Yellow Coatie	93
Lassintullich – or Steer the Gill	58
Lea Rig, The - or An Oidhche a Bha Bhanais Ann	5
Lees of Luncarty, The	93
Leith Hall	156
Lennoxlove to Blantyre	136
Leslie	52
Lick the Ladle Sandy	13
Lieutenant A. Stewart	18
Limerick Lasses	70
Link Him Doddie	10
Little Donald's Wife – or An Gabh Thu Bean, A Dhò'ill Bhig!	42
Liverpool Hornpipe	170
Loch Derculich	107

Loch Earn	87
Loch Ericht Side	27
Loch Glassie	59
Loch Ruthven	162
Lochan A' Chait	105
Lochend Side	133
Lochiel's Rant	108
Lochrynach	100
Lord Airlie	154
Lord Alexander Gordon	16
Lord Blantyre	21
Lord Dalhousie	59
Lord Down	134
Lord Eglintoun's Auld Man	68
Lord Elphinston – or Ca' Hawkie Through the Water	49
Lord Glenorchy	138
Lord Hay	81
Lord James Murray	76
Lord John Campbell	73
Lord Kelly	127
Lord Kilmaurs	108
Lord Kinnaird	63
Lord Lovat's Welcome	146
Lord Lyndoch	71
Lord Lyndoch's Welcome	26
Lord Macdonald	67
Lord Macdonald	89
Lord Moira	139
Lord Ramsay	119
Lord Saltoun	17
Lord Seaforth	88
Lord Strathaven	146
Lovat's Restoration	74
Macfarlane's Rant	67
Mackenzie's Rant	44
Maclauchlane's Scotch Measure	182
Macvicar's	32
Mad Cap	118
Maid of Islay	147
Maids of Islay, The	13
Màiri Bhòidheach	138
Major McBean	15
Major Molle	45
Maoile Nan Crogaichean – or Orkney	77
Marchioness of Huntly	38
Marchioness of Huntly , The	12
Marchioness' Salute, The	151
Marnoch's	51
Marquess of Lorn	76
Marquis of Huntly	127
Marquis of Huntly	149
Marquis of Huntly's Farewell, The	7
Marquis of Huntly's Highland Fling	60
Marquis of Huntly's Snuff Mill	154
Marquis of Huntly's Welcome to the Royal Highlanders, The	160
Marquis of Queensberry	29
Marquis of Tullibardine , The	7
Marry Me Now	49
Mary Gray	88
Mason's Apron	3
Meg Merrilees	176
Meg Mhór Na Lurachan	111
Menzies Rant	79
Merry Lads and Bonny Lasses	151
Merry Lads of Ayr, The	28
Merry Making, The – or A' Chridhealachd	136
Merry May The Pair Be	16
Mill of Laggan, The	138
Miller Lads	140
Miller of Camserney, The	25
Miller of Dron	6
Miller's Daughter, The	79
Miller's Man, The	71
Miss Abercromby	166
Miss Ann Amelia Murray	140
Miss Ann Stewart, East Craigs	135
Miss Austin	125

Miss Baird of Saughton Hall	150
Miss Betsey Robertson	90
Miss Betty Hunter	38
Miss Caroline Campbell (Reel)	122
Miss Caroline Campbell (Strathspey)	122
Miss Charters	130
Miss Clementina Stewart	133
Miss Colston	22
Miss Colston	126
Miss Cox	161
Miss Davidson	145
Miss Douglas	99
Miss Douglas of Springwood Park	84
Miss Drummond of Megginch	37
Miss Drummond of Perth	43
Miss Dumbreck	119
Miss Dundas of Arniston	76
Miss Elenora Robertson	118
Miss Erskine of Alva	20
Miss Erskine of Tony	152
Miss Fleming of Killiechassie	9
Miss Fogo	92
Miss Forbes	33
Miss Forbes Farewell to Banff	179
Miss Forbes of Pitsligo	160
Miss Forsyth Huntly	50
Miss Gibson - or The Cumberland	114
Miss Grant of Grant	144
Miss Grant of Kinaird	160
Miss Gray of Carse	134
Miss Hamilton of Bangowrie	153
Miss Hay of Yester	76
Miss Henny Mackenzie	26
Miss Heron	146
Miss Hog, Newliston	125
Miss Hopkins	117
Miss Innes	112
Miss Jane Grant, Lynmore	157
Miss Jeffrey	24
Miss Jenny Guthrie	23
Miss Jessie Scott	70
Miss Jessy Cumming	79
Miss Johnston	73
Miss Johnston of Hilton (Reel)	110
Miss Johnston of Hilton (Strathspey)	161
Miss Johnstone	91
Miss Katherine Stewart Forbes	157
Miss L Montgomrie of Skermorlie	118
Miss Louisa Duff	133
Miss Lyall (Reel)	48
Miss Lyall (Strathspey)	48
Miss M. Ross	113
Miss Macdowal Grant of Arndilly	165
Miss Macinnes	158
Miss Mackenzie of Gairloch	45
Miss Maclean	128
Miss Macleod of Colbeck	160
Miss Macpherson Grant of Ballindalloch	142
Miss Margaret Campbell (Saddell)	23
Miss Margaret Graeme of Inchbrakie	130
Miss Maria Dundas	91
Miss Maria Dundas	153
Miss Mary Macdonald	125
Miss Mary Stewart of Derculich	64
Miss Maule of Panmure	36
Miss May Hay	107
Miss Menzies of Culdares	1
Miss Menzies of Menzies	123
Miss Moneypenny of Pitmilly	127
Miss Muir Mackenzie	168
Miss Murray of Auchtertyre	143
Miss Nancie Low	156
Miss Nisbet of Dirleton	47
Miss Pensy Macdonald	102
Miss Rattray	55
Miss Robertson of Tullybelton	124
Miss Rose	19

Miss Ross	23
Miss Ross	121
Miss Sarah Drummond of Perth	110
Miss Scott of Usan	155
Miss Sitwell	120
Miss Stewart of Grantully (Reel)	2
Miss Stewart of Grantully (Strathspey)	1
Miss Stewart, Bunrannoch – or Ciorsdan Mhór	113
Miss Stewart-Robertson of Edradynate	137
Miss Susan Gordon	147
Miss Taylor	40
Miss Vere Hay	116
Miss W. Macdowal of Arndilly	39
Miss Wardlaw	161
Miss Watt	122
Miss Wedderburn	1
Miss Welsh	142
Miss Whitefoord	117
Miss Young	39
Mo Laochan Bòidheach	60
Mo Mhàiri Mhin, Mheall-Shùileach	51
Montgomerie's Hornpipe	170
Monymusk	85
Moray Club, The	73
Morpeth Rant Hornpipe	172
Moy Hall	32
Mr Baillie of Mellerstain	111
Mr Bernard	148
Mr Campbell Craignish	139
Mr Compton of Compton Hall	14
Mr Donaldson	123
Mr Douglas of Springwood Park	96
Mr Dundas Macqueen	167
Mr Dun's Frolick	153
Mr George Anderson	102
Mr Grant of Glenquaich	78
Mr Gray of Carse	35
Mr Gun Munro of Poyntz-Field	38
Mr James George	38
Mr James Hamilton	159
Mr John Smith	161
Mr John Stewart of Grantully	24
Mr Lumsden	146
Mr Menzies of Culdares	65
Mr Moray of Abercairny	128
Mr Robertson of Lude	77
Mr Thom	132
Mrs Adie	114
Mrs Baird	126
Mrs Baird of Newbyth	37
Mrs Bourke	154
Mrs Brown of Linkwood	106
Mrs Campbell of Lochnell	35
Mrs Campbell of Monzie	133
Mrs Chisholm	15
Mrs Christie	49
Mrs Colonel Forbes	39
Mrs Colonel Neynoe	161
Mrs Crawford	81
Mrs Douglas Moncreiff	99
Mrs Douglas of Ednam	19
Mrs Drummond of Logiealmond	111
Mrs Duncan	164
Mrs Dundas McQueen	22
Mrs Dundas of Arniston	33
Mrs Forbes	5
Mrs Fraser, Cullen	123
Mrs Garden of Troup (Reel)	158
Mrs Garden of Troup (Strathspey)	137
Mrs General Campbell	49
Mrs General Maxwell	41
Mrs George Johnstone of Byker	83
Mrs Gillies	118
Mrs Gordon of Aberdour	100
Mrs Gordon of Belsies	148
Mrs Gordon of Whitehill	101
Mrs Hamilton of Wishaw	120
Mrs James Campbell	150
Mrs Kennedy of Greenan	109
Mrs Macdonald of Clanranald	107
Mrs Macdonald of Clanranald	116
Mrs Macdowal Grant	141
Mrs Macleod	129
Mrs Macleod of Ellanreoch	69
Mrs MacLeod of Gesto	160
Mrs Macpherson Gibston	165
Mrs McLeod	4
Mrs Menzies of Culdares	124
Mrs Moneypenny	36
Mrs Moray of Abercairny (Reel)	74
Mrs Moray of Abercairny (Strathspey)	74
Mrs Morthland	126
Mrs Morthland (Reel)	41
Mrs Muir Mackenzie	37
Mrs Mure of Caldwell	75
Mrs Norman Lockhart	155
Mrs Oswald of Auchincruive	99
Mrs Ramsay of Barnton	110
Mrs Ronald	156
Mrs Rose	100
Mrs Small	68
Mrs Stewart Fleming of Killiechassie	119
Mrs Stewart Nicholson	166
Mrs Stewart of Garth	159
Mrs Stewart, Inverugie	68
Mrs Tulloch, Earnhill	124
Mrs Wright	106
Mrs Young of Cornhills	159
Muileann Dubh	43
Mull Rant, The	84
My Wife's A Wanton Wee Thing	173
Neil Roy	130
Nether Cluny	120
New Mill of Logierait, The	50
New Year's Day	40
Newbyth House	110
Niel Gow	9
Niel Gow's Farewell to Whisky	182
Niel Gow's Lament for Abercairny	101
Niel Gow's Wife	126
Nighean Dubh Alasdair	18
Nighean Dubh Nan Geala Chas	95
Night We Had The Goats, The – or An Oidhche Bha Na Gabhair Againn	92
Nine Pint Coggie	105
North Bridge of Edinburgh	82
North Hunt, The	97
North of the Grampians	28
North of the Tay	113
North of the Tweed	113
Novelty, The	163
Null Thar Nan Eileanan – or America	6
O Gin Ye Were Dead Gudeman	182
O She's Comical	4
O Welcome to My Dearie O	97
O'er Bogie	31
Off She Goes	174
Old Dumbarton Drums	181
Old Isle of Mull Tune – or The Dervaig Medley	174
Old Man Will Never Die, The	101
Orkney	78
Orkney – or Maoile Nan Crogaichean	77
Ossian's Hall	15
Oyster Wives' Rant, The	47
Parks of Fochabers, The	149
Pass About the Flagon	132
Pay As You Go	46
Pease Strae	54
Peggie's Wedding	175
Peggy Menzies	85
Perrie Werrie, The	91
Perth Assembly	138
Perth Hunt, The	2
Perthshire Volunteers	3
Peter Baillie	105

Peter Reid	54
Petronella	180
Pipe Slang, The	44
Pirriwig, The	111
Pitnacree Ferryman, The	57
Poll an Droighinn	14
Port a' Bhodaich	5
Port Mor Na Lurgann	137
Port Na Cailliche	112
Port Nan Con – or The Bob o' Dooly	8
Pretty Peggy	56
Prince Charlie	106
Prince Charlie's Medley	173
Push About the Jorum	89
Rachel Rae	56
Rannoch Lodge	13
Reel of Tulloch	4
Rendezvous, The	97
Riefield Lodge	131
Rinettan's Daughter	44
Rise Ye Lazy Fellow	45
Roaring Jelly	174
Roaring Rivie	52
Rob an Lugi	22
Rob Roy Macgregor	108
Robert Menzies	20
Robertson's Hornpipe	171
Romp Among The Whins	23
Rory Macnab	109
Rory O'More	177
Rothiemurchus Rant	34
Rover, The	107
Row, The	81
Ruidhle Nam Maragan Dubha	59
'S Molanach	16
Saighdear Ruadh	87
Sally Kelly	140
Sanders Brane	144
Sandy Is My Darling	44
Sandy O'er the Lea	61
Scolding Wives of Abertarff, The	129
Sean Chaisteal Ghart	8
Sean Phort Maith	58
Sean Rong Mór	57
Seumas Mór A Ghlinne	137
Sgiandubh	175
Sheep Shanks	17
Sidh Chailinn	44
Sir Archd. Dunbar	68
Sir David Hunter Blair	154
Sir George Mackenzie	58
Sir John Lockhart Ross	132
Sir John Stewart of Grantully	159
Sir Reginald Macdonald	8
Sir Robert Peel	121
Sir Ronald Macdonald	130
Sleepy Maggie	83
Smith of Killiechassie, The	41
Smith's Burn, The – or Allt A' Ghobhainn	3
Sodger Lad	175
Soldier's Joy	181
Sound of Mull – or Crònan Na Linne Mhuilich	43
Source of Spey, The	92
Speed the Plough	9
Sportsman's Haunt, The	83
Square and the Compass, The	33
St. Kilda Wedding, The	10
Steer the Gill – or Lassintullich	58
Stewart's March, The – or Gabhaidh Sinn an Rathad Mór	181
Stewart's Rant, The	10
'Stoigh leam féin an Siosalach – or The Chisholm	142
Stool of Repentance, The	172
Stormont Lads, The	87
Strathbogie Toast, The – or The Bobers of Brechin	127
Strathearn	129
Stratherick	115
Strathmashy	163

Struan Robertson's Rant	104
Stumpie	8
Sucky Bids Me	95
Susie Brodle	97
Swallow, The	52
Sweet Molly	104
Symon Brodie	109
Taigeis Agus Dealg Innte – or The Haggis	29
Tarbolton Lodge	103
Teviot Bridge	172
Theàrlaich! Nan Tigeadh Tu! – or Flora Macdonald	104
This Is No' My Ain House	66
Thorn Bush	20
Tigh An Dùin	109
Tigh Eachainn	98
Tigh Iain Ghròit – or Johnny Groat's House	36
Timour the Tartar	25
Tobar Mo Bheatha	61
Torry Burn	86
Triumph, The	176
Tullochgorum	86
Tullymet Hall	50
Tweeddale Club, The	34
Uist Lasses' Darling, The	73
Up and Waur Them A' Willie	11
Urquhart Castle	115
Viscountess Duncan	77
Waking of the Fauld, The	90
Walking of the Plaiding, The	159
Wandering Tinker	34
Wappinschaw, The	144
Waterloo	180
Weaver's Daughter, The	135
Wedding Ring, The	133
Welcome To Your Feet Again.	28
Wests Hornpipe	169
Wha Wad'na Fecht for Charlie..	85
What's A' the Steer	179
Whigs of Fife, The	152
Whipman's Rant, The	62
Whisky Welcome Back Again	121
Whistle O'er the Lave O't .	94
White Cockade, The	178
Will Ye Run Awa' Wi' Me	46
Willie Davie .	176
Willie Duncan .	35
Wind That Shakes The Barley, The	56
Yester House	17
Yetts of Muckart, The	25

GAELIC TRANSLATIONS

Gaelic	English	Page
A' Chridhealachd	The Hilarity (Of The Scene)	136
A' Chuachag	The Little Drinking Cup	67
A Dhòmhnuill, A Dhòmhnuill	Donald! Donald!	87
Alasdair MacAlasdair	Alexander's Son	43
Allt A' Ghobhainn	The Smith's Burn	3
An Bodach Luideach Odhar	The Dun, Slovenly Carle	63
An Gabh Thu Bean, A Dhòill Bhig!	Will Ye Take A Wife, Little Donald?	42
An Gearran	A Lower Ridge Of Feargan Hill	53
An Gille Dubh, Mo Laochan	The Black Laddie, My Darling	53
An Oidhche A Bha Bhainais Ann	The Wedding Night	5
An Oidhche Bha Gabhair Againn	The Night We Had The Goats	92
As, A Thòiseach	Be Off, Macintosh!	106
Baile Nan Granndach	Grantown	75
Biodag Air Mac Alasdair	Macallastair Wears A Dirk	19
Biodag Air Mac Thòmais	Thomas' Son Wears A Dirk	2
Biodag Dhòill-Ic Alasdair	Glengarry's Dirk	14
Briogan Seambo	Chamois Breeches	85
Cabar-Féidh	Deer-Horns	27
Caisteal Chuimri	Comrie Castle	90
Calum Figheadair	Weaver Malcolm	151
Calum Breugach	Lying Malcolm	48
Carn Dubh	The Black Cairn	8
'Chailleach Mhùsgach	The Blear-Eyed Old Woman	19
'Chailleach Odhar	The Sallow Old Woman	54
'Chailleach Oidhche	The Owl	22
Chuir I Glùn Air A' Bhodach	She Put Her Knee on the Carl	46
Ciorsdan Mhór	Big Kirsty	112/113
Clach Na Cùdain	The Stone of the Tub (Inverness)	60
Coille An Togail	The Brew-Wood	127
Coirechoille	The Wooded Ravine (Braemar)	82
Creag Na Pollaich	The Rock Overhanging the Marshes	31
Crònan Na Linne Mhuilich	The Moaning of the Sound of Mull	43
Croughly	(Croughly) Gordon's Reel	157
Domhnull Cléireach	Donald Clark	74
Druim-Uachdair	The Higher Ridge	86
Dubh-Chnocan	Blackhills (Strathtay)	61
Feargan	A Hill in Strathtay	43
Gabhaidh Sinn An Rathad Mór	We'll Take the High Road	181
Gille Calum	The Lad Malcolm	4
Ladar Mór A' Ghogain	The Big Ladle of the Cog	106
Lochan A' Chait	The Cat's Little Loch	105
Màiri Bhòidheach	Pretty Mary	138
Maoile Nan Crogaichean	The Old Ewes' Hill Pasture	77
Meg Mhór Na Lurachan	Big Romping Meg	111
Mo Laochan Bòidheach	My Bonny Darling	60
Mo Mhàiri Mhin, Mheall-Shùileach	My Gentle, Winning eyed Mary	51
Muileann Dubh	The Black Mill	43
Nighean Dubh Alasdair	Alexander's Dark Haired Daughter	18
Nighean Dubh Nan Geala Chas	The Black-Haired, White-Footed Maid	95
Null Thar Nan Eileanan, Dh'america Gun Téid Sinn	Beyond The Islands, To America We Go	6
Poll An Droighinn	The Thorn Pool	14
Port A' Bhodaich	The Old Man's Tune	5
Port Mór Na Lurgann	Lurgan's Great Tune	137
Port Na Cailliche	The Old Wife's Tune	112
Port Nan Con	The Dogs' Tune	8
Ruidhle Nam Maragan Dubha	The Reel of the Black Pudding	59
Saighdear Ruadh	The Red Soldier	87
Sean Chaisteal Chart	Old Garth Castle	8
Sean Phort Maith	A Good Old Tune	58
Sean Rong Mór	A Big, Old, Lazy Man	57
Seumas Mór A' Ghlinne	Big James of the Glen	137
Sgian Dubh	A Black Knife	175
Sidh Chailinn	The Maiden Breast	44
'S Molanach	Abounding in Hillocks	16
'Stoigh Leam Fhéin An Siosalach	My Choice is, The Chisholm	142
Taigeis Agus Dealg Innte	A Haggis and Skewer (In It)	29
Theàrlaich! Nan Tigeadh Tu	Charlie! Would you only come	104
Tigh An Dùin	The House of the Hill	109
Tigh Eachainn	Hector's House	98
Tigh Iain Ghròit	John O' Groat's House	36
Tobar Mo Bheatha	The Well of my Life	61